His Faithful Word
Applies

His Faithful Word Applies

Danielle Hope

Library of Congress Control Number: 2019908798
ISBN: Hardcover   978-1-7960-4395-2
                 Softcover   978-1-7960-4394-5
                 eBook   978-1-7960-4393-8

Print information available on the last page.

Rev. date: 07/01/2019

To order additional copies of this book, contact:
Xlibris
1-888-795-4274
www.Xlibris.com
Orders@Xlibris.com
799008

CONTENTS

Acknowledgement ix

Introduction xi

Chapter 1   It's a Choice, Bondage or Freedom 1

Chapter 2   Be Humiliated or Be Humble 4

Chapter 3   Do Not Lose Heart...9

Chapter 4   Know His Love, Trust His Love 13

Chapter 5   Call Me Grumpy or Call Me Grateful 18

Chapter 6   The Three C's That We All Run From 22

Chapter 7   A Grateful Heart; a Thankful Heart.............................26

Chapter 8   I Will Deliver You from Things Unseen 30

Chapter 9   Be Merciful and Forgive 35

Chapter 10 His Word, His Will, His Way.......................................40

Chapter 11 An Intimate relationship with God 43

Chapter 12 Grace 46

I have seen it come alive!

Acknowledgement

I would like to thank my Husband and
daughter for always loving me.

And a special thanks to my dear friend *TC* that
spent many hours helping me type this book.

Introduction

My Testimony

Mary had an advantage as a soon to be mother that no other mother has ever had. She was told by an angel that her child would be the Savior of the world. Each one of us who hold our babies for the first time have no idea what that child is destined for. But Mary had a purpose that we can all have as parents. To know the Lord through His word, do His will and be all that we can be. This is the most important legacy we can give them as parents. Are we raising teachers, doctors, ministers or maybe even a president? We have no way of knowing unless we pray for our child each day and seek God's will for their life. He will reveal His plan. When you decided to keep your child and raise it, you gave that child an advantage I did not have.

When my mother was 15 years old she became pregnant with a baby girl. At the age of 16, she became pregnant again with another baby girl. My grandmother told her she could keep one child but not the other. I was that second child. I was placed in a foster home as a child of the state until I was 14 months old. At that time, a couple took me home as foster parents. They wanted to adopt me but it took four years for the adoption to go through.

I still remember the day at the courthouse even though I was so young. The judge put me on his knee and told me that I was special because most children do not get chosen, but I was chosen. Today I can say that it was a wonderful way to encourage a child, but it took me many long years to see that I had the advantage God chose for my life. I felt rejected, unloved, and never good enough. I spent half of my life feeling unloved and making many bad choices. I was always striving to be good enough and loved the way I thought I should have been loved.

As a teen I was a wild child wanting so much to be accepted. As a young adult, at the age of 21, I married someone that I had loved since I was sixteen years old. I was not looking for God's choice for me. I never knew at that time that God's choices would be so different from mine. But the Lord can make good out of everything. When I was 32 years old, I had a back injury that put me in bed for 10 months. My husband's precious grandmother gave me a Bible and since I could not get up to do anything else, I devoured it as I read the scriptures. I read how much Jesus loved me and had a plan for my life. I learned that even if my mother did not want me God had a plan for my life. I learned that Jesus died on the cross for my sins and my past was forgiven and I only had to believe and ask Him into my heart. I did exactly that and my life began to change dramatically. My back was healed, I started to attend church and I got involved with my church family. I began to write music for the Lord and sing my heart out for Him.

God was preparing and cleansing my heart from the inside out. The feeling of rejection continued for another seven years. Then, one day the marriage was over. At that time, I asked the Lord how He could love me, as no one else did. I was overweight and had a very low self-esteem. The day my husband left, the Lord gave me the scripture Psalm 25:3, "No one who puts their trust in God will ever be ashamed..." (New International Version)

As the Lord continued to show me He had a plan, I clung to the Lord tighter than ever and for the next ten years He filled my life with purpose, building a music ministry and helping others. I sang in prisons, hospitals, nursing homes, taught voice lessons and became a choir director. The list of where the Lord led me is endless. God healed my heart and taught me that if God is for you, who can be against you.

In the latter part of 1998, a prophet came to our church. He prayed over many people and had a word for many individuals. When he came to me he said, "I don't have a lot for you but the Lord told me to give you this dollar and for you to keep it as a promise that your finances are going to change." I still have that dollar! Then he said, "I see you moving somewhere and next spring I see you walking through a meadow of flowers. I was very perplexed. Where was I moving and what meadow? Well, I met my soon-to-be husband in a prayer group and by the next April we were married and on our honeymoon in Switzerland holding hands and walking through a meadow. My finances did change. I paid off all my debts and became determined to always pay my tithe and give back to the Lord all I could of myself. And yes, I did move into my new husband's home.

I share this because of how awesome the Lord can work in our lives. But I caution people to be careful when people say they have a word from the Lord for you. We had much prayer, counseling and confirmation before we were married.

My second husband was a gift from God. The Lord spoke that to me on my wedding day. He was a widow. He is a man of God who treats me with the love and respect God intended for a woman. He prays for me and with me. He loves me unconditionally. We serve the Lord in ministry together and combined our families like the Brady bunch. I have a beautiful daughter from my first marriage and a son and daughter from my second marriage. We have beautiful grandchildren now and our lives are very full. I thank God for His many blessings and that He had a plan for me. We all have the opportunity to let our children know God and know His love, to not feel rejected or walk a sinful path of regrets.

One of my favorite songs has the words "His deep, deep love washes all my sins. His deep, deep love fills a need within." I have experienced that love. His faithful Word guides me each day. It is my heart's desire to share some of those experiences with you. To encourage you that His Word is faithful. His Word is true. We can learn and stand on it through every area of our lives.

Chapter 1

It's a Choice, Bondage or Freedom

Bondage keeps us from walking in the will of God. Lord, I pray that you would help each and every one of us choose freedom over bondage in our lives, in Jesus' name.

Do we choose to be walking in the direction of God's Word or the bondage of the enemy? We need to realize that sometimes the enemy is ourselves and the choices that we make. The spirit that we feed is the one that will survive.

The scripture that most fits this chapter is Exodus 6:9 (NIV). The Israelites did not listen to the Lord because they were in the bondage of slavery and discouragement. The Lord has given me four points that fall under bondage.

We do not listen or trust God when we are discouraged. When we look at our bank balances, our job situations or maybe even the lives of our children, are we trusting that God is in control or are we trying to make things happen in our own strength until we become weak, tired and broken? Are we praying or are we complaining? Are we, trusting His Word that says God will provide what we need or are we listening to the lies of the enemy that get us all tied up in knots? Believe me when I say these are things I have not mastered. I am a work in progress and my stomach knows all about knots.

What we choose to be doing can keep us bound up and keep us from hearing God. It could be computers, our favorite TV shows or other forms of entertainment like our IPhones. We may be so obsessed with our jobs that the important things in life just pass us by. Are we so busy driving our children to all the activities we think they need to be involved in that we are not taking time to pray with them or read the Word to them? If we choose these things over reading His Word, how can we hear His voice or His will for our lives? We tell ourselves we are too tired or we just do not have the time. But yet when we do read His Word we find comfort and peace. When we do take the time everything does fall into place. Are we making ourselves available to God or just following our own flesh?

Fear keeps us from choosing to do what is best for us. The Israelites needed to listen to Moses who heard from God, instead of people and circumstances that held them back from stepping out and receiving the Promised Land. Forty years in the desert taught the people to have faith in who God was and what He wanted for them. We all have to walk in the desert until we are willing to learn what God wants to teach us. This is our choice.

Fear often keeps us from walking into the unknown. Entering a new year is like entering unchartered territory. Fear of the unknown can cripple our capacity to follow God's leading through the days ahead. But if we are like Abraham, who clung to the One who knows all things, we are in good hands regardless of where He leads us. Psalm 34:4 says "I sought the Lord, and He answered me; he delivered me from all my fears." (New International Version) Think about that for a minute. <u>All my fears mean each and every one of them</u>!

My husband, and I had to take a trip to California to sign the completion papers on our rental that had been flooded by a broken pipe. We were to inspect the repairs and sign off on them. The weather was very terrible at the time and we were not sure if we should drive the eleven hours to San Jose possibly facing rain and snow.

We asked for prayer in addition to seeking God ourselves. We asked God to tell us not to go if it was not safe and when to go if it was safe. We were scheduled to leave on Thursday morning. God said "No" to both of us very clearly. Sure enough, the weather was very dangerous that day. Then we prayed and asked God if we should leave late Friday and drive halfway, get a hotel and drive the rest of the way on Saturday, but on Friday morning, the Lord spoke to both of us, "Go Now!" I was confused and afraid because my daughter was very upset that we were leaving. She felt like we were not being responsible when all the weather reports were against us traveling. I told her that God had said "Go" so we needed to trust that God knew what was best for us more than she did.

Needless to say, she was not happy. I have learned in my walk that our children need to learn and have their own testimonies in life. I began to pray in the Spirit and as we drove toward the dark clouds ahead an amazing thing happened. The clouds separated, each and every one, all the way to San Jose! It was like the parting of the Red Sea! Later that evening, there was another storm. Had we waited, we would have been in the midst of it.

When we arrived, we received a multitude of blessings. The house was completed very nicely and we signed off on everything. We saw our grandchildren and went to a dear friend's wedding. We also went to a mega church in town where we saw friends we had not seen in years. Last but not least, my husband and I had dinner at the restaurant where he had proposed to me. The time was very special, but knowing that God helped us and directed our path was invaluable.

Hebrews 11 gives us a challenge. It tells us that Abraham obeyed when he was called. Abraham trusted God and, went not, knowing where he was going. Galatians 5:1 (NIV) says, "It is for freedom that Christ has set us free. Stand firm, then, and do not let yourselves be burdened again by a yoke of slavery." Slavery is bondage, but we can choose to be free!

Chapter 2

Be Humiliated or Be Humble

When we are humiliated our dignity is reduced and our pride is brought to a lower position. When we are humble we are meek, modest, unpretentious and at times even lowly. What does the Lord want you to choose for your life?

I really felt like this chapter needed to be addressed at this point because from my own experience I have learned that unless we humble ourselves before God we have a long road ahead as you will see later on.

Since I was a little girl, I was taught and even encouraged to stick up for myself, to fight for issues, stand up to people and not let others push me around or those that I cared about. It was ingrained in me to the point that my father would say "No daughter of mine is going to let anyone get away with that." He made me feel like I should be ashamed or embarrassed if I let anyone try to tell me anything, saying "Well, who do they think they are?"

For over 30 years, the Lord has been speaking to me just the opposite. Through His Word and His Holy Spirit, He has been gently nudging me, but lately it is more of a PUSH instead of a nudge. I feel like God is helping me to see beyond the scriptures that He has a plan and it is not just about obedience to His Word. It is about trusting that he truly has a plan for <u>all</u> of us.

The main text for this chapter is Ephesians 4:2-3 (NIV), which says, "Be completely humble and gentle; be patient, <u>bearing with one another in love</u>. Make every effort to keep the unity of the Spirit through the bond of peace."

<u>There is no peace without humility</u>!

Our natural instinct is to always argue an issue or tell our side, so to speak. But in Titus 3:2 (NIV) it says "to slander no one, to be peaceable and considerate, and to show true humility toward all men," not just the ones who are kind to us. To the rest of the world this may seem crazy, but we need to have Faith in God and express love to others. Jesus said, Matthew 11:29 (NIV), "Take my yoke upon you and learn from me, for I am gentle and humble in heart, and you will find rest for your souls."

<u>Gentle words turn away wrath</u>!

Recently, I went to get my nails done by the lady who regularly does my fills about every two weeks. She noticed that my toes had a different design and asked me where I had them done. I told her it was at a new place in town that does hot rock pedicures. They put hot steaming rocks on your feet as they massage them. I will not go into all the details but she came unglued and started screaming at me how she wanted to do my nails and my feet and that she had already lost two other clients to the same place. She yelled, "Why didn't you just let them do your hands too?" She went on and on making a scene and it was very ugly and embarrassing. I tried to tell her that she is the only one I like to do my hands but because of the five surgeries that I have had on my feet, the hot rocks were very therapeutic. On the outside I remained very calm which was a miracle in itself. But on the inside, I was very upset and began praying for God to calm me so I would not say or do anything I would be sorry for. When I got into the car I said, "God, what just happened? Should I not go back there again? Should

I go somewhere else? I was a customer, how could she speak to me like that? Should I call her back and set her straight?" The Lord said, "Pray for her." I began praying for her and He showed me her fear of losing customers and her desperation. First, I prayed that God would increase her business. Then, I prayed that God would give her wisdom as to how to speak to customers. Then, I asked Him to let me know if I should go back again or just go somewhere else.

When two weeks had gone by and it was time for another fill, I went back, praying that God would give me wisdom if she started yelling again. She was flabbergasted when I walked in and I could tell a little embarrassed, but very happy I came back. As she did my nails, she was explaining that she was very tired because she had so many customers that morning. I told her that I had been praying that God would increase her business and she was very shocked.

I need to explain that at the last time she had done my nails, before the yelling incident, we talked about God and church. She said her husband was a Christian and she was a Buddhist. He was looking for a Christian church and she wanted to know about the church I attended. It was no coincidence to me what had happened when she blew up. The enemy was mad and did not want me telling anyone about God or church.

Well, she did my nails and this time she was a sweetheart and I really felt the peace of God over the situation. On Mondays, My husband and I do food delivery for the sick and elderly and we took her a plate. She was blown away. Psalm 25:9 (NIV) says, "He guides the humble in what is right and teaches them his way. Proverbs 3:34 (NIV) says he gives grace to the humble. It was only by His grace that I was able to go back there again. Colossians 4:6 (NIV) says, "Let your conversation be always full of grace, seasoned with salt, so that you may know how to answer everyone." Salt is a preservative and tasty. I am sure it makes situations easier to swallow. I am convinced that staying in the Word is pouring strength into me.

I had another incident recently where a woman was yelling at me because I was driving an electric cart, which I usually do in a grocery store because of my bad feet. She wanted the cart for her daughter who had a back brace. I apologized and took the cart to her daughter. This again was the Lord. The old me would have handled it quite differently. Philippians 2:3 (NIV) says, "Do nothing out of selfish ambition or vain conceit, but in humility consider others better than yourselves." Believe me, I have so much to work on in this area, but it is only by God's grace and the Holy Spirit that my mind has been opened like never before. We need the experience of submitting to one another in humility and love."

My husband and I went to a buffet restaurant for lunch after church one day. I was standing in a food line waiting to get a piece of chicken when all of a sudden a lady shoved me so hard she almost knocked me over. As she grabbed a piece of chicken, I said, "I'm sorry." She just looked at me and walked away. As she walked to her table, I began to laugh because I noticed at that point that she was so tiny and could not have weighed more than 90 lbs. and I was at least twice her size. I felt like God told me to have a sense of humor and not be so serious all the time. It is part of being humble. Be adaptable! We should never think that what we want is more important than what others want. For every minute you are angry you lose 60 seconds of happiness (Ralph Waldo Emerson).

Colossians 3:12 (NIV) says, "Therefore, as God's chosen people, holy and dearly loved, clothe yourselves with compassion, kindness, humility, gentleness and patience." Verse 13 states, "Bear with each other and forgive whatever grievances you may have against one another." Proverbs 15:33 (NIV) says, "The fear of the Lord teaches a man wisdom, and humility comes before honor." Isaiah 26:5 (NIV) says, "He humbles those who dwell on high, he lays the lofty city low; he levels it to the ground."

Many years ago, while my husband and I were doing prison ministry in San Jose, we were ministering to about 20 men in a barred, confined area. Across from that area was a solitary cell where one man was sitting on the ground listening. As we left that evening, the man sad to my humble husband, "Go to hell!" My husband did not hear him correctly and said, "Thank you!" I proceeded to say, "Do you know what that man just said?" When I told my husband what was said, he just said "No, really?" The next week we preached and the same man was in solitary again. The Lord must have really done something to his heart because as we walked by this time he said, "Thank you and God bless you! Jeremiah 31:19 (NIV) states, "After I strayed, I repented; after I came to understand, I beat my breast. I was ashamed and humiliated because I bore the disgrace of my youth."

I am going to share one more life lesson on humility. Years ago, I did nails and my specialty was pedicures. In the salon where I worked, Friday was two for one day and two ladies came in from the Santa Cruz, mountains to get their feet done together. My lady put her feet in the water as I was getting towels and when I laid her feet on my lap the towel turned black! There was so much mud in her nails that I had to cut it all away before I could even work on them. I felt like I was going to vomit but I prayed in the Spirit under my breath for strength to get through it. I worked on that lady for an hour and a half and when I finished her feet looked great. I told this story to my Elder's wife and she asked me why I kept working on this client. I told her it was because of the scripture to watch what you say or do, you might be entertaining angels. She laughed and said, "Do you really think angels would come in with feet like that?" I said, "I didn't want to take a chance!"

I want that attitude again, never knowing if I am entertaining angels and to humble myself in the sight of the Lord. I do not want to focus on myself and what I want, but to be considerate of others.

I am going to end this chapter with 2 Chronicles 7:14 (NIV), "If my people, who are called by my name, will humble themselves and pray and seek my face and turn from their wicked ways, then I will hear from heaven and will forgive their sin and will heal their land."

Chapter 3

Do Not Lose Heart

Discouragement is something that we all feel in our lifetime. It wears us down, makes us weak and at times makes us feel hopeless. We may feel anxious or restless because we want to make everything better. We want to fix it all when things become overwhelming. Ultimately, what we really want is peace, peace in our heart that everything is going to be okay.

Several years ago I found my life in a situation that caused me to be very discouraged. I asked myself the question, "Is this how it is always going to be?" I kept trying to hang on but I felt like there was a part of my life where I had no control. I am going to share with you why I was so discouraged and anxious, but before I do I want to let you know that My husband and I prayed about this at some length and feel that it is important to share. We hope it will encourage someone who also may be feeling discouraged and let you know we are all human.

As I said before, there was a time when our lives began to unravel. My husband was showing signs of Alzheimer's or dementia in things that he was saying and doing. I really panicked because my stepmother had died in my arms of Alzheimer's and before my father died he suffered from dementia after having a stroke. In addition to this, in the past I had knee surgery where the doctors put me on a medication that made me hallucinate and feel like I was losing my mind for about five months. Not being able to rationalize or function normally is very disheartening! I remember reading the Bible and praying that God would make the words on the page make sense to me again. I should have remembered God's faithfulness during those times in my life but instead I let fear creep in. I understand now that discouragement is really fear, when we have no control over a situation.

I love my husband so much and I was so frightened to see what was happening. I began to question everything that he did. The more anxious I got the more he was not himself because I was stressing him out. I prayed and I prayed and the Lord told me to get him to a neurologist. It took about a month to convince him to go. We had also found out that we were both diabetic and the doctors were trying to find the correct medication to get our sugar levels under control. This also makes a person anxious and confused. I will not go into all the things my husband was doing but I will focus on my fear and how the enemy made me lose heart and feel like our lives were falling apart.

The doctors did every test possible including an MRI on his brain. What they told us was that my husband did not have Alzheimer's. What he did have was a condition called MCI (Mild Cognitive Impairment). It involves problems with the memory, language, thinking and judgment that are greater than your typical age-related changes. It is like the beginning stages of dementia. There was a medication that they wanted to try that could slow the process down and even reverse it to some degree. Within 2-3 weeks I could see signs of my old My husband coming back, but by this time I had worked myself and My husband into an anxious state of mind.

God always knows what He is doing. My husband had to go to California for five weeks on family business with his children and work on our rental. I was so exhausted from mothering him that I don't know if I pushed him out the door or he just ran to freedom. Five weeks turned into seven weeks because he then had to go to Switzerland for a funeral. The medication for the MCI and the diabetic medication had plenty of time to take effect. He came home like my husband I had married and his A1C sugar level was down from 7.9 to 5.3, which is phenomenal! He was able to drive all the freeways in California, which is a feat in itself. He traveled planes, buses and trains without me. He did all the maintenance on our rental by himself with no one to assist him. God helped him to get his confidence back while his medication kicked in and God helped me to relax and know that God can do a much better job of taking care of my husband than I ever could. My husband was tested again and he only missed one point out of 30.

While My husband was gone I was determined that I was going to find peace in the scriptures and find a way to get back to trusting the faithfulness of God, the faithfulness He had shown me all of my life. As I opened my Bible, the Lord led me to Psalm 27:13-14, which in the New King James version verse 13 states, "I would have lost heart, unless I had believed that I would see the goodness of the Lord in the land of the living." Is there something in your life that you have lost heart about? Verse 14 states, "Wait on the Lord; be of good courage, and He shall strengthen your heart; wait, I say, on the Lord!" The Amplified version states, "What, what would have become of me had I not believed to see the Lord's goodness in the land of the living! Wait and hope for and expect the Lord; be brave and of good courage, and let your heart be stout and enduring. Yes, wait and hope for and expect the Lord."

WHAT WOULD BECOME OF US IF WE DID NOT BELIEVE?

How many of us are confident that we will see the goodness of the Lord? Do we believe all of God's Word or just parts of it? What really hit me was I would have lost heart.

Webster's Dictionary says that the heart is the source of life; the seat of emotions and affections, the inner part of anything. To lose heart means to despair. I have been reminded through God's Word that we all get discouraged, but we need to keep our heart stout and enduring for we know the hope we have in Jesus Christ!

I would like to share a few scriptures that the Lord has used to encourage me:

"The Lord is my light and my salvation - whom shall I fear? The Lord is the stronghold of my life - of whom shall I be afraid?" Psalm 27:1 (New International Version)

"Since ancient times no one has heard, no ear has perceived, no eye has seen any God besides you, who acts on behalf of those who wait for Him." Isaiah 64:4 (NIV) Are you willing to wait for Him?

Exodus 35:5 says, "...Whoever is of a willing heart, let him bring it as an offering to the Lord." (New King James Version) What better offering can we give Him than to be willing?

In 1 Samuel 16:7 it says "...For the Lord does not see as man sees, for man looks at the outward appearance, but <u>the Lord looks at the heart</u>." (NKJV)

"LET NO MAN'S HEART FAIL..." 1 Samuel 17:32 (NKJV)

In Deuteronomy 1:28 it states, "...Our brethren have discouraged our hearts..." (NKJV) Have you let people or circumstances discourage your hearts like I have? <u>Remember, the closer you get to God the smaller everything else appears</u>.

I used to stress out about things for days and days. Now it may only hit me for a couple of hours and sometimes when I am reading His Word it is only a few minutes before I feel the peace of God. When my husband and I worship the Lord together every stress seems to disappear.

We have determined that we will enjoy the years the Lord gives us and as the medication continues to work. But when and if that changes, we are confident that the Lord has a plan for that too!

I also encourage you to speak words of life to yourself and to others knowing that the God of Peace will crush Satan under your feet!

I found a wonderful poem by Michael Bright and I would like to share a few of my favorite lines with you.

Silver Boxes

My words were harsh and hasty and they came without a thought. Then I saw the pain and anguish that my bitter words had brought.

Bitter words that I had spoken made me think back through the past; of how many times I'd uttered biting words whose pain would last.

Then I wondered of the people I had hurt by things I've said; all the ones I had discouraged when I didn't use my head.

Silver boxes full of treasure, precious gifts from God above; that all the people I encounter might have a box of God's own love.

Chapter 4

Know His Love, Trust His Love

The main text for today is Ephesians 3:17-19. "...And I pray that you, being rooted and established in love, may have power, together with all the saints, to grasp how wide and long and high and deep is the love of Christ, and to <u>KNOW THIS LOVE THAT SURPASSES KNOWLEDGE</u> - that you may be filled to the measure of all the fullness of GOD." (NIV, emphasis mine)

As Christians we grasp and are even grateful for the knowledge that He loved us so much that He died for our sins. This love truly <u>does</u> surpass our own personal knowledge. How many times do we go through life trying to make things happen our own way instead of His way even though we know His way is better? After all, who else understands what we are going through better than we do? But true faith and trusting God has nothing to do with what we are feeling. It is about trusting that His plan for us truly is for our own good. Jeremiah 29:11 says, "I know the plans I have for you," declares the Lord, "plans to prosper you and not to harm you, plans to give you hope and a future." (NIV)

Isaiah 55:8 says, "For my thoughts are not your thoughts, neither are your ways my ways," declares the Lord. Do we really trust that His plans are better than ours? How many of us truly believe that? Psalm 40:4 says, "Blessed is the man who makes the Lord his trust...."

Proverbs 3:5 says, "Trust in the Lord with all your heart and lean not on your own understanding; in all your ways acknowledge Him, and He will make your paths straight." And in verse 7, "<u>Do not be wise in your own eyes</u>..." (NIV)

I am sure every one of us could recall areas in our lives where we were not trusting God, but trying to do it our way and make life happen. We begin that at an early age as a small child when our parents say don't touch the flame or we will get burned. How many flames have we touched and how many fires has the Lord had to put out for us with His mercy and His grace? God loves us so much that He allows us to experience the choices we have made. Like a child that is learning to walk, we have to stumble and fall until we get it right.

Speaking to women first, how many of us searched for that perfect husband? We wanted to be married so badly that we definitely made some bad choices along the way. When I think of my choices before my first marriage and before my marriage to My husband, I am amazed at how the Lord could love me when I did not love myself enough to seek God's perfect man for me. Many women marry alcoholics, abusers, cheaters, or ungodly men with no vision for God's plan in their lives. We have reaped the consequences of those choices. If a young woman came to me now and asked about dating or looking for the right husband, I would <u>not</u> say date and seek them out or try them on for size. That is the way the world thinks. I would say, be still and know that He is God (Psalm 46:10 NIV). Psalm 62:8 (NIV)encourages us to trust in God at <u>all</u> times. <u>All means ALL</u>! And though the world thinks it is a cliché, seek first His kingdom and His righteousness, and all these things will be given to you (Matthew 6:33 (NIV)).

Men, I am going to speak to you about finances. I say men because they are the head of the home, but as a once divorced woman, I learned many valuable lessons along the way. There are many women that are also the head of their household. Just remember, Christ is the Supreme head of every home!

After my divorce, I took part of my settlement and bought a townhouse. In seven months it tripled in value so I sold it and bought a beautiful four bedroom house with a lap pool. I really believe now that I went ahead of God. In California, if you sell a home at a profit before keeping it for two years you will owe the government a lot of money. I owed $20,000 in taxes for selling too soon. I remember using my credit cards to rob Peter to pay Paul. I took in renters to try to make a $1,800 house payment because I was not waiting on God to give me His best. I was trying to get it on my own. I ended up selling the house at a loss, filing bankruptcy, and living in a one room little house. Isaiah 30:1 says, "Woe to the obstinate children," declares the Lord, "to those who carry out plans that are not mine..." (NIV) Woe to me for my ignorance in not seeking God every step of the way. We are willing to seek God in some things but not willing to give Him everything! I am so glad that He chastises those He loves just like we do our own children. I thank God for Isaiah 43:2 that says, "When you pass through the waters, I will be with you..." (NIV) God was always there. He never left me. Many people who have had to file bankruptcy beat themselves up so badly that they do not know how to go forward. Isaiah 43:18-19 says, "Forget the former things; do not dwell in the past. See, I am doing a new thing!" (NIV) Learn from the past, do not dwell on it!

At this stage in my life I learned about tithing. I did not tithe or understand the concept of trusting God in this way. I did not understand that it all belongs to God. I believed that you took care of all your own needs and wants and if there was any leftover you might throw $10 in the offering. I was struggling so much emotionally trying to find happiness in worthless things after the divorce that I did not think much about tithing until my life seemed to be falling apart. Isn't that how we are though? We don't think much about seeking God's will until our life is falling apart. I began tithing in about 1995 and have remained tithing to this day. I truly believe this is the area that most people do not trust God, not believing His Word that tells us He will provide what we need. It is not up to us to do that. In Luke 16:10, it says, "Whoever can be trusted with very little can also be trusted with much..." (NIV) I had to learn to the hard way to be trusted with little and I am a living testimony that God has blessed me with more than I could have ever dreamed! Proverbs 19:21 says, "Many are the plans in a man's heart, but it is the Lord's purpose that prevails." (NIV) And Psalm 33:11 says, "But the plans of the Lord stand firm forever..." (NIV)

I also feel led to address health issues. God has healed me through 16 surgeries and several tumors including one in my breast that He miraculously healed in one day. The day God healed me He reminded me of the scripture that says, "Have you forgotten the miracles I have done and the things that I can do?" (Psalm 78:11 (NIV) paraphrased) We have access to awesome prayer warriors and I just cry with joy when I think of what God has done through prayers. There is nothing too big or too small for God. He cares, but we must share. Have you ever thought that the healings in your life are the testimonies that can bring others to Christ?

The last issue that God is dealing with in my life is trusting, God enough to wait patiently on Him. Psalm 40:1 says, "I waited patiently on the Lord; He turned to me and heard my cry." (NIV) Two words I struggle with are wait and patiently! Sometimes I feel like the Lord is slapping me alongside my head saying, "Danielle, do you get it yet?"

When, I looked up "wait" in Webster's Dictionary it said, "To stay in one place in expectation." Expectation! I could live with that. Then it said, "To put it off to a later date." Now there are times when I say, "Why Lord, why not now?"

The word "patience" according to Webster's Dictionary is "Uncomplaining endurance when under stress." Oh how my husband and God would love that!

Are you waiting with the weight of the world on your shoulders? Proverbs 11:1 says, "The Lord abhors dishonest scales..." Are we being honest with ourselves? It goes on to say, "accurate weights, are His delight." (NIV) Now think of that word "weights" as a pun for waiting honestly on God.

Romans 8:24 says, "...But hope that is seen is no hope at all..." (NIV) Who hopes for what he already has? But if we hope for what we do not yet have, we wait for it patiently. Hebrew 6:12 (NIV) says that through patience we will inherit what is promised. The more we study God's Word we will understand the awesome love of God! The more we understand how deep that love is, the more we will trust God in <u>every</u> area of our lives. The love of God compels us to do what is right.

I hope this has encouraged you that we are all human and struggle every day with trusting God, but through His Holy Spirit we can learn to trust God's love and put all our hope in His precious Son! God's Spirit anoints us to trust. His Spirit qualifies us and equips us. Amen!

Chapter 5

Call Me Grumpy or Call Me Grateful

Thank God that Christians are not perfect. We are forgiven, not because of who we are, but because of Jesus Christ who took our sins and nailed them to a cross with Him. We were the ones who deserved the punishment but He paid the price.

Although I have been a Christian for over 30 years, study the Word, pray and try to live my life serving the Lord, He is really speaking to my heart about cleaning up my act. He is zeroing in on those areas that do not witness the joy of the Lord. It is one thing to read His Word and another to know it in your heart. It is even more important to live it in our lives. God's Word truly is a lamp unto our feet!

The Lord gave me this message a while ago and He has been having me work through it daily. It is a work in progress, but so is our walk with the Lord.

In a previous chapter, I shared with you how God was dealing with my fears through my husband's condition of MCI (Mild Cognitive Impairment). God told me that he had it under control and that I should trust that He and the medication could take better care of my husband than I ever could.

Well, now God is speaking to me about grumbling and complaining. It would be so much easier if God just said, "Danielle, this is what you are doing, get it right!" But instead He wants me to share it with others, to BARE ALL, so that we may all take a good look at our lives and say, "Wow, am I doing that?"

I have to share with you a little about my past in order to explain the present. Not as an excuse, but to show patterns in our lives that we do not even recognize. Many people know that I was adopted, but what you do not know is that my adoptive parents spoiled me rotten! They let me have whatever they could afford and my own way about almost anything I wanted. As a teenager, I thought it was because they just did not care about me, because I really was not their real daughter. As an adult, I once asked my father why he let me be so wild and did not correct or punish me. His answer was, "We were afraid if we said no you would think we didn't love you." That answer blew me away but it also set a pattern. If you love me you will give me what I want or do it my way! My adoptive parents were so Loving and patient with me!

In my first marriage, my husband would buy me expensive gifts to make things right when we were at odds.

After being single for 10 years I was determined that I was going to do things my way and no one was every going to tell me how to live, again. God was my source and I did not need anyone to tell me what to do! Yes, God is our provider, but He wants us to do things His way. His way is so much better than ours and that kind of attitude in any relationship is totally not going to fly with God. It goes against all His scriptures of submission.

Then sweet my husband, comes into my life. He treats me like a queen. God told me that day we were married that he was God's gift to me. I will never figure out why God blessed me with such a man of God. He wakes me in the morning singing praises to God! He waits on me hand and foot and even makes my coffee in the morning.

I tell you all of this to share the pattern of "if you love me" had made me a spoiled child always expecting things my way and on my terms. Sometimes I say things and ask myself "why did I just say that? Why didn't I just say thank you?" My husband will surely have a crown on his head when he gets to heaven.

It's not how sweet and holy we sound when we are praying that matters. How are we speaking at home? That question really speaks volumes to me! The Holy Spirit said, "You've become a grumbler and a complainer!" Life, is not Burger King, we don't have it our way. Life is giving not just receiving. The Holy Spirit said, "I want you to do a study on grumbling and complaining." Webster's Dictionary says to grumble is to murmur with discontent. Complaining is to express dissatisfaction, distress or grief. The Holy Spirit said to me that my distress causes suffering on others. I need to be grateful. Most of us center on, what pleases us! When we are complaining we are not being content with God's will. If I am not believing and trusting God, I cannot please Him! God's Word is like a mirror where we have to take a good look at ourselves. I hear the Lord say to me, "What does my Word say?"

My main text for this chapter is Jude 16, "These men are grumblers and faultfinders; they follow their own evil desires..." (NIV) OUCH! How many times are we complaining for our own evil desires, just as the people of Exodus did? Philippians 2:14(NIV) says, "Do everything without complaining or arguing, so that you may become blameless and pure children of God..." Numbers 11:1(NIV) says, "Now the people complained about their hardships..." Are we going through a tsunami or starvation? What do we have to complain about? James 5:9(NIV) says, "Don't grumble against each other, brothers, or you will be judged. The Judge is standing at the door."

When we study God's Word and see ourselves through God's eyes it can be very frightening. That is when we need to remember 1 John 1:9(NIV), "If we confess our sins, he is faithful and just and will forgive us our sins and purify us from all unrighteousness."

One of my favorite scriptures is Hebrews 12:6(NIV), "because the Lord disciplines those he loves..." We can also go to Romans 8:1 which says, "Therefore, there is now no condemnation for those who are in Christ Jesus."

I once heard if we are complaining more than we are praying, we have a problem!

So after we confess our sin what do we do? 1 Thessalonians 5:16 (NIV) says, "Give thanks in all circumstances, for this is God's will for you in Christ Jesus." I somehow missed the word "all" circumstances, so I began thanking God for all the things he blessed me with and does for me. He then spoke to me very clearly, "The blessing is not in what I give you or getting your way. The blessing is that you know that I love you, in spite of yourself!" Thank you, Lord, that you love me enough to chastise me.

We all have anxiety. It is the legitimate cares and concerns of life, but if we trust God we will pray and give those cares to him. I know I will have my days, and so will everyone else, but we need to determine to give thanks for ALL things, in ALL circumstances, in ALL our little annoyances that don't even matter. As we thank Him with a truly grateful heart, our fleshly things will melt away. Psalm 30:11 (NIV) says, "You turned my wailing into dancing; you removed my sackcloth and clothed me with joy, that my heart may sing to you and not be silent. O Lord my God, I will give you thanks forever."

Chapter 6

The Three C's That We All Run From

There are two "C" words that everyone at some time or another has run away from. Those two words are "commitment" and "constant."

What is it about commitment that makes us shake in our boots? What are we afraid of? Let's look at what Webster's says about commitment. It means to entrust or pledge to, to <u>obligate or engage ourselves</u>, to bind by pledge or assurance. I like the German translation which says to <u>give over to or release to others</u>. What are some of the things we ARE willing to commit to? What are some of the things we ARE NOT willing to commit to? When we committed our lives to Jesus what were did that mean? I know the first and most important thing we commit to is to believe He is the Son of God and gave His life for our sins when He died on the cross, and because of His death our sins are forgiven and we will have eternal life with Him!

Let's look beyond that to 2 Chronicles 16:9 (NIV), "For the eyes of the Lord range throughout the earth to strengthen those whose hearts are fully committed to him..." (NIV) That is truly amazing to me that He is looking at my heart to see if I am truly committed to Him and if I am He will give me the strength to do what I need to do. If I will humble myself, I am acknowledging that <u>without Him I am without resource</u>. He will give me the strength and means to take each task into completion. Proverbs 16:3 (NIV) says, "Commit to the Lord whatever you do and your plans will succeed." Psalm 37:5-6 (NIV) says, "Commit your way to the Lord; trust in Him and He will do this: He will make your righteousness shine like the dawn, the justice of your cause like the noonday sun." Wow!

Now I would like to take this a step further and discuss the word "COMMITTEE." A committee is a group of people appointed to perform a task. We, the church, are a committee. What is our task? What are we <u>constantly committed</u> to do for the Lord? Are we to come and sit in church every Sunday and listen to the Pastor and go home? I believe <u>it is so much more</u> than that. Are we taking what we are hearing and applying it in our lives first and foremost? And second, what are we doing in our church to help keep it all together? Our Pastor is committed to preach God's Word and not change or try to put his own feelings into it. I have seen worship teams singing year after year to bring us into an attitude of worship. I have seen so many people committed to teach our children all about Jesus. So many workers committed to keep the body of Christ in unity and order by ushering, greeting, giving communion, and the list goes on and on. There are people who clean the bathrooms and vacuum the church year after year. There are people committed to raise up disciples. That is a commitment! What about tithing? Are we committed to give our tithe to the Lord? And I cannot go without saying there are awesome prayer warriors in our churches that have literally prayed healing over our families and our bodies. The healing has been incredible! That takes commitment.

We speak so much about how we want God to move in our churches and bring more people and how we want to be used of God yet all of this takes commitment. I know how busy all of our lives are, but I encourage you to seek the Lord and ask Him how He would want you to commit to your church body. And know that if He directs you He will give you the tools and show you the way. <u>Whatever we do in our church, it should be by the Holy Spirit and not out of obligation</u>!

Now back to God's Word. 1 Peter 4:11 (NIV) says, "...If anyone serves, he should do it with the strength God provides, so that in all things God may be praised through Jesus Christ." It does not say we should be praised, but God should be praised! Acts 20:32 (NIV) says,

"Now I <u>commit</u> you to God and to the word of His grace, which can build you up and give you an inheritance among all those who are sanctified." Are we committed to build others up? I Peter 4:19 (NIV) says, "So, then, those who suffer according to <u>God's will</u> should <u>commit</u> themselves to their faithful Creator and continue to do Good." What are we continuing to do good that is for the Body of Christ? Matthew 11:27(NIV) says, "All things have been <u>committed</u> to me by my Father..."

I cannot speak about commitment without speaking about the word "constant," which means to be steadfast, unchanging, unwavering in thought or deed, fixed, to <u>stand together, steady in action and purpose and affection.</u>

Hebrews 5:13-14 (NIV) says, "Anyone who lives on milk, being still an infant, is not acquainted with the teaching about righteousness. But solid food is for the mature, who by CONSTANT use have trained themselves to distinguish, good from evil."

I Chronicles 28:7 Says, "Moreover, I will establish his kingdom forever if he be CONSTANT to do my commandments and judgments as at this day." (King James Bible, emphasis mine)

Galatians 6:9 says, "Let us not become weary in doing good, for at the proper time we will reap a harvest if we do not give up." (NIV)

Matthew 7:16 says, "You will know them by their fruit." (NKJV) What fruit are we producing?

Philippians 2:13 says, "For, it is God who works in you to will and to act <u>according to His good purpose</u>." (NIV)

Ephesians 2:21-22(NIV) says, "In Him the whole building is joined together and rises to become a holy temple in the Lord. And in Him you too are being built <u>together</u> to become a dwelling in which God lives by His Spirit."

Intention, faith and obedience cannot be separated. We must be <u>committed</u>! We must be <u>constant</u>! 2 Timothy 4:7 (NIV) says, "I have fought the good fight, I have finished the race, I have kept the faith."

Finally, our goal should be to <u>be COMPLETE IN CHRIST!</u> James 1:4 says, "Perseverance must finish its work so that you may be mature and <u>complete</u>, not lacking anything." James 2:22 (NIV) says, "You see that his faith and his actions were working together, and his faith was made <u>complete</u> by what he did."

In John 17:23 (NIV) Jesus said, "...May they be brought to <u>complete</u> <u>unity</u> to let the world know that you sent me and have loved them even as you have loved me."

Acts 20:24 (NIV) says, "...if only I may finish the race and <u>complete</u> the task the Lord Jesus has given me - the task of testifying to the gospel of God's grace."

As I close I would like to share a prayer that God put on my heart and as I read it to you I hope that this message will place a specific prayer on your heart.

Lord, in place of a bad attitude, give, me a thankful heart. In place of impatience, give me compassion and forbearance. In place of worry and fear, give me trust and hope in you. In place of rudeness and anger, give me a caring heart, a listening ear and a willingness to give it <u>ALL TO YOU</u>!

Chapter 7

A Grateful Heart; a Thankful Heart

I was doing my morning devotional and reading a scripture from Joyce Meyers book "Love Out Loud." The scripture was 2 Corinthians 9:15 (NIV). It said, "Thanks, be to God for His indescribable gift!" As I read it I said to the Lord, "Thank you, Lord, for all your gifts to me." I heard the Lord Say, "Are you grateful?" I said, "Yes, Lord." Then He said, "What are you grateful for?" I started to name off things, "Thank you for my husband, my children, my grandchildren, my home, my church family and all the times you have healed me." Then the Lord said, "Yes?" I said, "Oh yes, Lord, thank you that you died on a cross for me so that I would have forgiveness and life with you forever!" I became overwhelmingly convicted that the outward things overshadowed what Jesus did when He gave His life. I was reminded that we become so caught up with the things we pray for each day, that we just let them distract us from what is REALLY important, the love of Christ! That love that we did not earn and don't even deserve! The love that is unconditional. The <u>free</u> gift, that is there, if only we will <u>receive</u> it.

My main text for this chapter is Colossians 3:16. "Let the word of Christ dwell in you richly as you teach and admonish one another with all wisdom, and as you sing psalms, hymns and spiritual songs with gratitude in your hearts to God." (NIV)

The Lord reminded me of the first few years after I received Christ over 30 years ago, how I used to say "Praise God and thank you Jesus" for everything in my life. I could literally see Jesus in everything. I praised him so much that I was reprimanded at work for making my boss and customers feel awkward at the nail shop where I worked. Then the Lord opened the door for me to have a nail shop behind my house in a room that was an in-law Quarters before my parents died. I received the blessing of talking about Jesus all the time and praying with my nail customers over the table like a bartender does in a bar, but the Spirit that was present was the Holy Spirit not alcohol. One customer said to me, "When I walk in this room I feel God."

I want to see Jesus in every situation every day in my life with gratitude in my heart. I went to the dictionary to get a handle on the word "gratitude" and it said it is a feeling or showing appreciation of kindness, thankful appreciation of benefits received. I know the benefits of forgiveness, salvation and the blessed Holy Spirit! But how do I show appreciation? I know that the Lord knows my heart but how do I live it with my life? It begins with believing but it should NEVER END THERE!

As I was researching gratitude and some special points stood out to me. And as they did the Lord gave me scripture to back them up.

Point #1 Happiness can come from a grateful heart. As Christians we know that happiness is the joy of the Lord. Psalm 30:11-12 (NIV) says, "You turned my wailing into dancing; you removed my sackcloth and clothed me with joy, that my heart may sing to you and not be silent. O Lord my God, I will give you thanks forever."

Point #2 Gratitude can help me through my worries and fears. The song "It is well with my soul" comes to mind. Colossians 3:2 (NIV) says, "Set your mind on things above, not on earthly things."

Point #3 Sleeping. If we are focused on appreciation of God's daily blessings I believe we will rest in Him. Colossians 3:15 (NIV) says, "Let the peace of Christ rule in your hearts.

Point #4 My <u>Health.</u> Thanking God for who He is has gotten me through every physical challenge I have been through. Psalm 107:1 (NIV) says, "Give thanks to the Lord, for He is good; his love endures forever."

Point #5 <u>Relationships.</u> This is so very important! It starts with our relationship to God then with our spouses, our children, with our grandchildren, and with our friends. Many times My husband says to me, "Thank you for cooking my dinner." Something most husbands take for granted but it makes me feel appreciated. I tell my husband, "Thank you for making my coffee" or "Thank you so much for praying with me. You really lifted me up! You always support me and encourage me." With friends I would like to say to my friend *Louise*, "Thank you for being my friend for over 40 years and my prayer partner!" To my friend *Violet*, "Thank you for always, being a listening ear and a prayer warrior." To my friend, *D*, I Say, "Thank you, for always seeing the positive, and always being willing to forgive people!"

One day I was at the church sewing the chairs that had ripped and a sister came in to clean the church. She saw what I was doing and said "Thank you for taking the time to do this for the church!" That really meant a lot to me. I said to her, "Thank you for keeping our church clean!"

With my daughter I try to tell her often, "Thank you for being so smart and helping me through this problem. I just didn't quite know how to do this or that but you really helped me." Have you noticed that the older we get the more we feel like we are the children and our children are the parents? They keep us up on all the latest things. With my grandchildren I often say, "Thank you for the kisses and hugs and thank you for making me laugh."

Now the reason I have said so much about regarding relationships is so that we acknowledge that <u>the Lord is the source of all our relationships</u>! He not only gave us life but all the precious people in our life! He even gives us the difficult people in our lives so that like a diamond in the rough we become polished and all He wants us to be.

I am so grateful for the Lord's forgiveness that I want to always forgive others and always Share his kindness. Colossians 3:17(NIV) says, "And whatever you do, whether in word or deed, do it all in the name of the Lord Jesus, giving thanks to God the Father through Him." What a blessing and joy it is to share with others all that the Lord has given me!

I would like to share a few more scriptures that we can apply to show the Lord our appreciation to His kindness and all His benefits.

Psalm 7:17 (NIV) says, "I will give thanks to the Lord because of His righteousness and will sing praise to the name of the Lord Most High."

Psalm 95:2 (NIV)says, "Let us come before Him with thanksgiving and extol Him with music and song."

I Thessalonians 5:18 (NIV) says, "Give, thanks in all circumstances, for this is God's will for you in Christ Jesus."

And finally, Psalm 100:1-5 (NIV), says, "Shout for joy to the Lord, all the earth. Worship the Lord with gladness; come before him with joyful songs. Know that the Lord is God. It is He, who made us, and we are his; we are his people, the sheep of His pasture. Enter His gates with thanksgiving and His courts with praise; give thanks to Him and praise His name. For the Lord is good and His love endures forever; his faithfulness continues through all generations."

LET THE REDEEMED OF THE LORD SAY SO!

Chapter 8

I Will Deliver You from Things Unseen

How many of us go through life thinking if I can see it, touch it or feel it I can control it? We don't like the unseen or the unknown. We back away from those things we do not have control over. We tend to stay away from unchartered territory in our lives. We forget that whatever we face in life we are NOT alone. GOD IS WITH US! We forget about the scripture that says, "Everyone who calls upon the name of the Lord will be saved." (Romans 10:13) (NIV) That does not mean only for salvation. We can and should call upon Jesus in every area of our lives.

I experienced a series of events that forced me to face the unseen and recognize that I was not alone and that the Lord was with me every step of the way. It started when my husband and I were babysitting in California at our home that we rent to my husband's daughter and son-in-law. They were on vacation and we were there to babysit our grandchildren for five days. The baby was down for her morning nap and the boys were playing with grandpa so I decided I would go upstairs and take a shower while I had the time. As I stepped into the shower, the water was ICY cold and it would not get warm so I wrapped up in a towel and went into the shower in the master bedroom. As I stepped in, it too was ICY cold! I thought, well I don't have a choice, just take a cold shower! As I was getting out my husband came upstairs to check on me and I told him about the water. He went down to check the water heater and went through all the steps that were written on the outside. At the end it said if these steps do not work to call the PG&E. If you are not from California, that means Pacific Gas and Electric Company. Well, the pilot light would not come back on so I called the PG&E. While I was on the phone, my husband came in and said there was a faint smell of gas at the meter outside. The gas company was not going to come that same day until my husband said there was a smell, then, they decided to come between noon and eight in the evening. Can you believe that? They also said do not turn anything on or off that wasn't already on until they got there as it could ignite the gas. Well, a freaked out grandma I became. Should I take the kids out of the house until eight or what should I do? Just then I got a severe pain in my stomach that doubled me over. I tried to get through giving the children lunch and kept praying for safety as I put the baby in her playpen. As she was playing with her toys, the pains became more severe so I just lied on the couch next to her. I just prayed and prayed. I knew I needed to go to the hospital but I did not want to leave the children until I knew the gas problem was fixed so that I would know they were safe. I called my other daughter-in-law because I knew she would get off work at 3:30. I asked her if she would stay with the kids so my husband could take me to the hospital. The gas man came at about three and by the time my daughter-in-law got there he had fixed the problem.

God's timing is always perfect! God knew about the gas problem and He knew I was going to be sick. We did not know about the gas problem but God alerted us with my cold shower. I did not know I was going to get a viral infection that would put me in the hospital for four days and a month of rest but God knew. How did I get it? Was it something unseen on the plane? Someone I had come in contact with? I don't know. There are people and unseen things we come in contact with every day but God knows all. He says in his Word that He will not leave us or forsake us. My scripture for this chapter is Deuteronomy 31:6 (NIV). "Be strong and courageous. Do not be afraid or terrified because of them, for the Lord your God goes with you; He will never leave you nor forsake you."

God wants to do wonderful things in our lives, but we must grow spiritually in Him. In the hospital, I had so many needles in me I thought I was going to lose it, but as I asked for prayer I literally felt the prayers that were lifting me up. I felt very powerless in the hospital. I was 700 miles from home, my husband had to stay with the children and my daughter was eight hours away in Las Vegas. But as I felt the prayers, I began to expect and believe that God was healing me!" I knew and believed I would be well again. I know that there are people who die from the flu and I know that at my age diabetes added to my weak state, but my God is greater. For when I am weak He is made strong within me!

The first weekend back home from California I was washing a load of clothes and our sewer line backed up all over the laundry room and all of our sinks, tubs and toilets. It was disgusting! I was in no condition to clean any of it but God knew it was going to happen. My daughter, who, was visiting that weekend called a plumber who arrived right away. It was fixed in one hour on the 4th of July weekend. That was a miracle! My husband, my daughter and son-in-law cleaned, bleached and sterilized everything in like three hours. It was amazing! I had to just calm down, bite the bullet and see how God was in control. I was so hard to sit there and not be able to do anything!

God was telling me I don't have to fix every situation. He is God and He has got it covered! There are many stories of people who have an unseen experience when God was there in the midst and knew all along what needed to be done. People who could not start their cars only to find out about an accident on the freeway that he kept them from. Our weaknesses show us how much we need God and how much He is there in our life. It reveals areas that needed to be dealt with. Yes, He truly chastises those He loves. I have tried to think of what my fears were that I had to face through all of these things and these came to mind.

1. I had a fear regarding safety but I was reminded that God knew about the gas leak and He was the one to alert us. He is all knowing!

2. I had a fear of dying alone because I was so ill. My husband had to stay with the grandchildren and my daughter was 600 miles away in Las Vegas. But I was not alone, God was with me!

3. The Lord revealed my fear of letting people down and not being there for them. I had made a commitment to take care of our grandchildren, but when I got sick I just had to trust God!

4. Next, was my fear of not being, a responsible person. How was I going to be able to come back, cook for people, do the church finances and decorate the church, for the 4th of JULY? These were all silly things that went through my head but God just said, "Danielle, are you serious? You need to rest for a month!"

5. God wanted me to face my cleaning phobia about germs, especially, after being sick. God was probably smiling while I had to sit and watch everyone else clean the sewer backup.

6. Last but not least, was my fear that if I were to die my daughter would be, alone. Like a lot of divorced women, we carry the guilt when our husbands leave, that our children's lives are our responsibility. It is ridiculous! First of all, they have God! And in my daughter's case, she also has a husband.

Life goes on and we will always have situations that we cannot see the outcome or understand that God has a plan. My daughter has two beautiful children that I love and worry about, so much at times it makes me feel physically ill. But that is what the enemy wants, he wants to incapacitate us. So I quote this scripture over and over again to myself, "Trust in the Lord with all your heart and lean not on your own understanding; in all your ways acknowledge Him, and He will make your paths straight." (Proverbs 3:5-6 (NIV)) I love God's Word!

I would like to share one more story of an unseen situation when God was truly in control. This story occurred many years ago but I was reminded of it recently. I am sure God was saying I never change; yesterday, today or tomorrow, I remain the same.

There was an Indian pastor that came to my church to share a story about his life. He was about 25 years-old and was going to speak in a country where Christianity was forbidden. It was going to take place in a large arena under strict control with guards all around. As he was getting ready, he could not find his white robe that he always wore when he spoke. He became very agitated because some of his luggage was missing. He called the airlines and hotel front desk to no avail. Finally, He decided to just wear regular street clothes. He prayed and asked God to forgive him for his temper and to guide him by His Holy Spirit as he ministered in the arena. As he spoke to the people, the anointing of God came down and many people came forward for the altar call. One man fell to his knees and cried "Forgive me, forgive me." Pastor said "God forgives you, you are forgiven." But the man said "You don't understand. I am a guard and all of the guards were instructed when the man with the white robe steps onto the stage shoot him! We give our hearts to Him and ask you to forgive us!"

Was it a coincidence that the Pastor could not find his white robe? No. God knew and he protected him. How many things in our life upset us because they did not go the way we had planned? I recently heard that this same Pastor is still preaching all over the world many, many, years later!

Whatever you are going through be encouraged this day that you are not alone. God is with you and he has a plan. Maybe, we just to reminded, to trust him in <u>ALL</u> situations.

Chapter 9

Be Merciful and Forgive

The topic the Lord has given me to speak about in this chapter is forgiveness. The Bible dictionary says that forgiveness means to pardon. So I take that to mean we should pardon our offenders the way that the Lord has pardoned us. The Lord says I am free from guilt or shame because of what He did on the cross for me. It also says to absolve one from condemnation. That tells us not to condemn a person with our words. The Bible tells us to speak words of life not death. We can speak blessings or curses over another human being. How often do I think about that when I speak?

Forgiveness means to exonerate, which is to cease to feel resentment against another. Wow, that is a tall order to cease to feel resentment. Therefore, I should not play mind or heart games with another human being to try and make them feel bad. I am to remove the liability, the debt I think they owe. I am to cover it with the love of Jesus. I am to release the offense and let it go, I am to show mercy. My grandson runs around the hose singing "Let it go! Let it go!" Now I know that comes from the movie "Frozen," but maybe through that song the Lord is trying to tell us something. I am sure He is speaking to me. I had said last time I spoke that I try to remember that the Lord forgave me but who am I not to forgive. And I truly have thought of that often. But God has shown me that I am not there yet! God has shown me that it is easier to believe this when we don't have our <u>pain in our face and reminders all around us</u>.

The main scripture for this chapter is Matthew 6:12, "And forgive us our debts, as we also have forgiven our debtors." (NASB)

Now the Lord is taking me to the next step. In the last few years, my ex-husband decided to leave California, retire and move to this town. He used to come once a year to see his father, play golf and see our daughter. I have tried to figure out why, out of 50 states in the U.S., he had to choose this place to retire, but I guess it is one of those things I don't need to understand. It is interesting that my father-in-law came to our church a couple of times for plays we had performed. Before he died, our pastors prayed with him to receive Christ. My husband, prayed with him the day he died to ask Jesus to take him home. In his instructions regarding his death he wanted his service to be held at our church. Our pastor spoke and several ladies made sandwiches and goodies and served food. I know that my ex-husband was very touched by the love of the people and how they served him and his family. I believe in my heart God was touching his heart.

Isaiah 55:8 says, "For my thoughts are not your thoughts, neither are your ways my ways, declares the Lord." (NIV) God knows what He is doing. He has His reasons and always has a plan. He had a plan with Esau when his birthright was stolen by Jacob and he fled. After, returning to his homeland in Genesis 33:4 (NIV) Esau ran to meet Jacob and embraced him. In verse 10, Jacob said to Esau, "For to see your face is like seeing the face of God, now that you have received me favorably." It was forgiveness that shown through. <u>Do we want our past offenders to see the face of God in us</u>?

Joseph said to his brothers who had sold him into slavery, "And now, do not be distressed and do not be angry with yourselves for selling me here, because it was to save lives that God sent me ahead of you." (Genesis 45:5(NIV))

I remember when the Lord brought me to here in 1993. He wanted to heal my heart and begin a music ministry in my life. He wanted to show me that I had value and He had a plan for my life. Then the Lord sent me back to California to meet and marry my husband. God always has a plan! I believe God wants me to forgive my ex-husband and allow him to <u>see the face of God through my life.</u> As I am studying forgiveness I find that you must be humble to be forgiving. That is a very overwhelming task before me if I listen to the enemy. I know that there have been a lot of changes especially on the holidays when my ex-husband wants to now spend them with our daughter. But the Word tells me the Lord will give me the tools to get through this too.

The second thing I am reading is that forgiveness must be from the heart. I will pray for the love of Jesus in my heart and remember that when <u>I am weak He is made strong in me</u>. Psalm 78:38 says, "But he, being compassionate, forgave their iniquity and did not destroy them;" (NASB) Psalm 25:11 says, "For your name's sake, O Lord, pardon my iniquity, for it is great." (NASB) Psalm 103:12 says, "As far as the east is from the west, so far has He removed our transgressions from us." (NASB)

Part of our hesitation to forgive is our fear of being hurt. We have to pray and ask God to help us not make the same choices and decisions that got us hurt in the first place. Isaiah 43:18 says, "Do not call to mind the former things, or ponder things of the past. Behold, <u>I will do something new</u>, now it will spring forth; will you not be aware of it? I will even make a roadway in the wilderness, rivers in the desert." (NASB)

Recently, the Lord reminded me of two more areas of forgiveness I need to address. I share this because I feel we have all experienced these moments when we do not want to forgive. The first is when someone has hurt someone I love very much. The Lord showed me I was hanging onto the resentment I had toward someone that had hurt a dear friend through infidelity and divorce. As God quickened that person to my heart, I began to pray and I realized I was still very angry. So I prayed for God to forgive me and help me to give that person to God. As I did, God reminded me that that person would have to stand before God for what he had done. I felt very sad for him and my anger was gone. <u>Do you know someone who has hurt someone you love</u>? I know if it was my own child who had been hurt I would need the Holy Spirit to really bring me to my knees to help me to forgive.

The second area the Lord showed me is to forgive people who lie. My husband has shared before how that is an absolute no-no to me since I was a child. My husband asked me where that came from and I really do not know, it was the way I was raised. If you know me you know the only time I will tell a lie is about a surprise party to get someone there. Even then I feel terrible! But the point is it is futile. Everyone around us lies, the government, people we know who try to cover their sin, etc. It is everywhere! I said to my husband, "How does God put up with us. He sees everything. He knows everything!" What came to both of us is God's mercy. What hurts the most is not that someone has lied to me. It is that people I love lie to themselves, suffer consequences and then wonder why they are in a particular situation. Again God said to me, "Just pray for my truth to set them free." God knows my weaknesses but I take comfort knowing that His Word gives me the strength to be an overcomer.

I have read in the Encyclopedia of the Bible that there are two types of forgiveness. The first one is human forgiveness like we have for each other as Joseph had for his brothers. There is also divine forgiveness. Divine forgiveness is implied rather than stated. Abel was accepted by God. Enoch walked with God. Noah was singled out as righteous and Abraham was known as a friend of God. David was known as a man after God's own heart. That is my deepest desire to be a child after His own heart. Mark 11:25 says, "Whenever you stand praying, forgive, if you have anything against anyone, so that your Father who is in heaven will also forgive your transgressions." (NASB)

To understand forgiveness we must also understand the judgment of God. Joseph said to his brothers, "Am I God to judge and punish you? God turned into good what you meant for evil." (Genesis 50:19-20, the, Living Bible) The Lord said to Moses, "When I come to visit these people I will punish them for their sins." (Exodus 32:34, the Living Bible) Many people want to punish others for their pain; they want to make the offender suffer. I shudder to think of those who must stand before God. I do not wish that on anyone! In 2 Corinthians 2:7 it says, "Now is the time to forgive him and comfort him. Otherwise he may become so bitter and discouraged that he won't be able to recover." (The Living Bible)

Most people that offend us know what they have done seconds after the offense. I believe God quickens that to people <u>even if they are unsaved</u>. But if we condemn and discourage them will they accept the God of love and forgiveness that we know?

Ephesians 4:31-32 says, "Get rid of all bitterness, rage and anger, brawling and slander, along with every form of malice. Be kind and compassionate to one another, forgiving each other, just as in Christ God forgave you." (NIV)

Colossians 3:13 says, "Bear with each other and forgive whatever grievances you may have against one another. Forgive as the Lord forgave you." (NIV)

If we are living in the light of God's presence, just as Christ does, then we have wonderful fellowship and joy with each other. I know that by the world's standards this is insane, but in Jesus there is forgiveness of sin. <u>HIS WOUNDS HAVE HEALED US</u>! (Isaiah 53:5 (NIV))

The Lord has given us such wonderful mercy. I know He wants us to be kind to someone who has treated us harshly. Mercy and forgiveness go hand-in-hand. So many times <u>in our flesh</u> we think, but that person has to suffer like I suffered. That is not mercy. It is also <u>God's decision</u>. He sees the picture so much more than we do. Matthew 9:13 says, "But go and learn what this means: I desire mercy, not sacrifice. For I have not come to call the righteous, but sinners. (NIV) James 2:13 says, "Because, judgment without mercy will be shown to anyone who has not been merciful. Mercy triumphs over judgment!" (NIV)

Charles Stanley said, "Even though believers may feel pain, anger or a desire to show revenge, they <u>choose to trust the Lord</u> to protect them and direct the outcome

I close by saying to myself, as well as everyone else

Let It Go! Let It Go! Give it all to God!

Chapter 10

His Word, His Will, His Way

I have shared in the past of how I had a back injury and was unable to walk for many months. How my ex-husband's grandmother gave me a bible and because I could do nothing else, I read and read and read! The word of God healed me, and set me free. It gave me new life. Psalm119 verse 1 ASV says, "Your Word is a lamp unto my feet and a light unto my path." God's word helps me guard myself when I am grounded in His word. His word is a truth I can always believe and hold onto so that I may grow in my walk with Him. I have learned that when I know God's Word and apply it to my life He can better protect my heart from the lies of the world. We need that so much in this day and age. The media tries so hard to win us over. His word lifts my spirit when I'm down, and it helps me strive to live the values He has set before me. I love the psalms they give me comfort. When I read them I feel God's Strength, and His encouragement. I believe His word is like love letters to His children. 1 Corinthians 7:35 NIV says, "I am saying this for your own good, not to restrict you, but that you may live in a right way in undivided devotion to the Lord. It makes me sad that the people who do not know Jesus and His word think He is trying to take things away from us, when in fact He loves us and just wants to protect us!

Webster's dictionary tells us that will is desire, intention, choice, pleasure. His will for us is His desire and pleasure. Matthew 6:10 NIV says, "Your Kingdom come your will be done." That should be the desire we all have for Jesus.

John 15:10 NIV says, "If you keep my commands, you will remain in my love, just as I have kept the Father's commands and remain in His love." That sounds like such a tall order but we cannot do this in our own strength but by His Holy Spirit, that came to live in our heart on the day that we asked Him in. Matthew 19:26 NIV says, "With man this is impossible, but with God all things are possible." When we desire God's will above all else, life becomes less overwhelming. We are not pushing ourselves to make things happen and we have the freedom of putting our lives in His hands, knowing His will is always what is best for us. Don't miss the joy of giving our worries to God and seeing His presence working in our life.

Matthew 11:29 NIV says, "take my yoke upon you and learn from me, for I am Gentle and humble in heart, and you will find rest for your souls." Let us remember the example and Love that Jesus set before us on the cross. Luke 22:42 NIV says, "Father if you are willing, take this cup from me; yet not my will, but yours be done.

Let us look at the final desire the Lord has set for us. His Way! His way is the course and road He has set before us. We may not always Understand, His methods but that's all right because Father God always knows what is Best! John 14:5 NIV says, "I am the way and the truth and the life. No one comes to the Father except through me." Isaiah 48:17 ESV says, I am the Lord your God, who teaches you the way you should go. " Isaiah 43:19 NIV says, "I am making a way in the wilderness.

What is so important in life that keeps us from following this course? I look back at my own stubbornness and think life could have been so Much, easier If, I had lived these words. When we read about the people in Exodus, I'm sure we can think of times we were so rebellious. In Exodus19:21, the Lord said to Moses, "Go down and warn the people so they don't force their way and many of them perish." When I read this I am embarrassed and very grateful for the mercy of God! I pray that someday I can quote Psalm 18:21 NIV "For I have

Kept the ways of the Lord; I am not guilty of turning from God." And in Colossians1:6 NIV In, <u>God's way</u>, is the gospel bearing fruit and growing throughout in my life since I read it so many years ago?

His Kingdom Come, His will be done on earth as it is in Heaven.

Chapter 11

An Intimate relationship with God

Fullness in life only comes when we truly experience God's love for us. When, we experience an Intimate relationship with God He sees our Hearts, and His heart is revealed to us through His word in so many, Ways. I have learned that in myself I am nothing but in Jesus I am Everything, I need to be. I have shared over the years that when I received the Baptism of the Holy Spirit that was the day that Jesus poured out his Love all over me, and I knew that love personally. When I accepted Him as Lord, and Savior, I understood that He loved us so much that He gave His only son, for our, forgiveness. The word us, was a group thing and not personal. Somehow that didn't Hold, the same weight with me. I was hurting and I needed to believe that He loved me! I had been told that morning, "Look at you, how, could anyone love you?" But that evening when I received the Baptism His overwhelming Love poured all over me, and I knew He really loved me, Danielle personally! He knows my heart. He listens to my prayers and in many cases already has the answers before I even ask. Since that time I have learned that love is something that needs to be rekindled. Not by God because his love never fails, but by me._Like in any relationship Love takes work. It is something we cannot take for granted. When you truly love someone, you give them all of_you and the return is overwhelming with the Lord.

How many movies have we watched that the character says, "You complete me?" They use these lines like "You give me purpose." Another dialogue I often hear is, "You make me a better person."

Now I like a good love story like any other woman, but the world doesn't understand, about the greatest intimate relationship of all is with Jesus Christ. Psalms 16:11 (NIV) says, you make known to me the path of life; you will fill me with joy in your presence, with eternal pleasures at your right hand. NIV Have we set our minds to pursue the purpose of God passionately? I ask this question of myself? What is my passion? What, are each of us, individually, passionate about? What gets our heart and our adrenaline going?

As I was researching the word intimate one of the explanations was devoted. Ask yourself the question, who, or what am I devoted to in my life? I am sad to say that in this world many people are devoted to themselves. Another explanation of intimacy was, without boundaries. Are we guilty of setting up boundaries and only allowing the Lord in certain areas of our lives? How can we be intimate with Him if we don't give him every part of ourselves? As I am writing this I really have to give this some thought in my own life. I know now why the Lord put this so heavy on my heart. One of my favorite thoughts regarding intimacy was that when we honestly being intimate with God we are within each-others minds. Does that sound strange? Think about your spouse or best friend. Are their times when you feel like you can finish each-others words? 1 Corinthians 2:16 (NIV) says, "For who has known the mind of Christ?" The answer is we have the mind of Christ, if He is in us and we are in Him. Romans 15:5 (NIV) says, "May the Lord who gives endurance and encouragement give you the same attitude of mind toward each other that Christ Jesus had." Romans 15:6 (NIV) says, "So, that with one mind and one voice you may glorify the God and Father." Romans 12:2 (NIV) DO NOT conform to the pattern of this world, but be transformed, by the renewing of your mind.

There are certain things we must do to give our mind over to God.

1. Remove those distracting things, in our life, that keep us from hearing His voice. TV, cell phones etc.
2. We, have to be sure we want His will above all else
3. Don't give up praying and trusting that His timing is the best.
4. Stand on His promises
5. Know that when you are in His will a peace will come.

In looking up relationship the word dependence came up. Am I depending on the Lord and not others in every area of my life? Only God can work on our hearts from within if we take all of our heart to Him. It's, natural that we don't want to go through adversity in our lives but Adversity helps purify our faith and helps us grow and even produce fruit. He is molding us and trusting Him is the only way to get over our fears.

Isaiah 41:10 says, "So do not fear for I am with you; do not be dismayed, for I am your God, I will strengthen you and help you. Is there any intimate relationship that can do all these things for us? Nothing can top our relationship with the Lord.

I remember the 10 years before I married my second husband my husband. Adversity taught me to depend on God. I learned to trust Him f0r all my needs. But even if we are married our most important relationship should always be with the Lord. Yes He knows our heart, our thoughts, and our fears. He is omniscient! He knows all things. He is Omnipresent. He never leaves us!

Let our highest priority be our relationship with God!

Chapter 12

Grace

As I look back over the years of my walk with the Lord, I am so thankful for His love, His forgiveness and His faithfulness! But at this time of my life I am most aware of His grace, for it is truly by His grace that I have lived my life. I can look back and see that He always had a plan and that I have never been alone. He has always been with me. Thank you, Most Loving God!

The main text for this message is Ephesians 2:8-9. "For it is by grace you have been saved, through faith - and this not from yourselves, it is the gift of God - not by works, so that no one can boast." (NIV)

Merriam-Webster Dictionary says, "Grace is an unmerited divine assistance given humans for their regeneration or their sanctification. I went on to look up regeneration and it said spiritual renewal or restoration of body or body part. It also says sanctification is God's will for us. So by His blood the Lord has given us a new life set apart to live for Him. It is not only His will that none should perish, but also He gives us His grace to live that new life through Him.

Grace is a gift we receive that we cannot buy or do anything to have. It is a power that comes to us through God to overcome the things we could never do on our own or in our own strength. His grace gives us the Knowledge to understand that is it Him and only Him helping us overcome.

It means so much more to me knowing that I cannot earn it through prayer, reading the Bible, going to church or any other works. It is receivable not buyable. Without the power of God's grace I would not be here writing these words to you and sharing my heart. Without His power I would not be able to sing to you of His love. Some people call that power the anointing of God. I only know I am grateful that I can do nothing without Him.

I remember once a lady had been invited to a Bible study who was a violinist. She came to a Care and Share where the church was giving out food. She was working her way through states to play her violin for the Philharmonic Orchestra. There was a room full of ladies and we were worshiping God singing "Holy Spirit, Thou art welcome in this place." She was not a Christian and had never heard the song before but she took out her violin that she carried everywhere and began to play. The power of God came upon her and every woman in the room could feel the presence of God. Was it her gifting of being a violinist? No, it was the Lord working through her. I would like to believe that at that moment she realized that playing the violin that day, was not of her own but that the unknown power of God was working through her. At the end of the bible study ladies prayed with her. God always has a plan.

We all know of people that preach or sing or serve in church ministries but the power of God is not upon them because they do so in the flesh and not by the Spirit. We can really distinguish the difference if we have a relationship with God. How many times in our lives have we gone through situations and thought "I can't do this." But we can do all things through Christ who strengthens us. How do we survive divorce or loss of a loved one in our lives? It is God's grace giving us the power. How do reformed addicts become overcomers? It is the grace and power of the Holy Spirit.

I used to be a three-pack a day smoker from the age of 13, but when I received Jesus in my heart I saw an image that if I put another cigarette in my mouth I would be putting it in the mouth of Jesus. The power of God came on me so strong that I threw away the three packs of cigarettes I had bought that morning and never smoked again.

The Lord desires for us to grow in Faith and in the Character of Jesus. In 2 Corinthians 12:9 (NIV), it says, "...My grace is sufficient for you, for my power is made perfect in weakness."

I would like to share more grace scriptures to encourage you.

Hebrews 4:16 (NIV) "Let us then approach the throne of grace with confidence, so that we may receive mercy and find grace to help us in our time of need." Some translations say come "boldly and fearlessly." I really like that.

John 1:14(NIV) "The Word became flesh and made His dwelling among us. We have seen His glory, the glory of the One and Only. Who, came from the Father, full of grace and truth."

John 1:17(NIV) "For the law was given through Moses; grace and truth came through Jesus Christ."

Zechariah 12:10 (NIV) "And I will pour out upon the house of David and the inhabitants of Jerusalem a spirit of grace and supplication."

I was thinking of how God's grace gave Moses the power to lead God's people out of Egypt and how God's grace gave Joseph strength and guidance to endure all that he did to save His family and brothers who had betrayed him. Think about poor Noah and the grace it took for him to build an ark with no water in sight! Do we ever think of the grace it took for Abraham to be willing to sacrifice his son on the altar and the <u>faith to believe</u> he must trust the Lord no matter what? We need to pray and ask God to give us that <u>attitude of faith</u>. And we can never forget the grace it took for Mary to endure the beating and death of her precious son, Jesus.

Is the Lord placing something on your heart that you need to go forward with in your life? Know in your heart if it is the Lord God's plan for you He will give you the grace. You can call it power, tools, wisdom, strength or open doors, whatever it takes, just know He has a plan.

Ask the Lord to show you the times in your life that it was only by His grace that you survived. Do you keep a prayer book or journal? I am sure everyone here could look back on God's grace in your life? Keep the promises of His Word in your heart always and speak to Him forever in prayer. I know that as long as I am here on this earth my faithful God will show me His grace.

I thought I was through with this word on grace but the Lord has been speaking to me very strongly regarding grace to others. Especially with my impatience with people who do things slower than I would like or not the way I would like. How I need to allow the power of God to work through me to show grace to others. I need to be more patient by His Holy Spirit. I need to not allow, my flesh to rise up, not in my power but by His Grace. Isn't it our goal to be more like Jesus? Then we need to show grace.

I am going to share with you a very embarrassing situation the Lord spoke to me regarding this. Embarrassing because of my attitude, but grateful because He chastises those He loves!

This week after our company left I was out in the casita changing all the bedding and towels and getting it ready for the housekeeper. I was very hot and tired when I finished and was on my way back into the house and realized my husband had locked the door. I knocked, banged and yelled but to no avail. It was the day the temperature was 113 and I was in my bare feet. I could not go back into the casita because I had locked it when I finished. Also, the front gate was locked so I was stuck. Instead of praying I banged and yelled till the dogs let my husband know I was there. When he finally opened the door I was yelling like a crazy woman. My husband did not say a word and went back to what he was doing. As I entered the house I realized my sweet husband was shampooing the carpets and that is why he did not hear me. How many times do we lose it not knowing the circumstances instead of praying and asking the Lord to help us?

I know my impatience with poor my husband drives him crazy and it is not showing grace. I am definitely a work in progress. But thank God He is not finished with me yet. Asking the Lord to help us be led by His Holy Spirit daily can help us be more gracious to others.

Can you think of areas in your life when you have not shown grace to others? Ask the Lord to guide you and allow the power of God to show you grace but also teach you to be gracious to others.

I am going to close with Jude 1:24-25, "To him who is able to keep you from falling and to present you before His glorious presence without fault and with great joy - to the only God our Savior be glory, majesty, power and authority, through Jesus Christ our Lord, before all ages, now and forever more! Amen.

The Sun and moon shall pass away
But my word shall live forever.

Thank you, Jesus, your word is true!

CPSIA information can be obtained
at www.ICGtesting.com
Printed in the USA
BVHW081519080719
552848BV00007B/158/P

9 781796 043952